# THE GOLFER'S PRAYER BOOK

## Walking the Fairway with the Master

Dorothy K. Ederer

HiddenSpring

The scriptural quotations used for each "hole" are taken from the New Revised Standard Version: Catholic Edition Copyright © 1989 and 1993, by the Division of Christian Education of the National Council of the Churches of Christ in the United States of America. Used by permission. All rights reserved.

Caseside design by Sharyn Banks
Author photo on back of book by Rachel Lindley
Book design by Lynn Else

Library of Congress Cataloging-in-Publication Data

Ederer, Dorothy K.
    The golfer's prayer book : walking the fairway with the master /Dorothy K. Ederer.
        p. cm.
    ISBN 978-1-58768-059-5 (alk. paper)
    1. Golfers—Prayers and devotions. 2. Golfers—Religious life. 3. Golf—Religious aspect—Christianity. I. Title.
    BV4596.G64E338 2010
    242'.68—dc22

                                                                        2010000925

Published by
HiddenSpring
an imprint of Paulist Press
997 Macarthur Boulevard
Mahwah, New Jersey 07430

www.hiddenspringbooks.com

Printed and bound in the United States of America

# CONTENTS

## Part Three: Readings Adapted from the Old Testament

## Part Four: Psalms for the Golfer

## Part Five: Vision-Inspired Prayers

I dedicate this book to the Master, who has been my unseen Companion in every game. Along the way, he arranges my lifetime companions, who see my game worthwhile whether I am winning or losing. These treasured golf companions in my family are: great nephew RJ and his parents, Colleen and Rob Galacz; Gerri and Joe Navarre; Jeanne Murphy; greatniece Kayleigh Schneider; Jenny Murphy; Bernard Ederer; and David Ederer. I met an expert on the course, Dee Wilson, club champ for twenty-two years, who became a dear friend and golfing coach.

I also dedicate this book to my dear friends, Kristin and Dan Dolsen, and Amy and Mike Cattell, for their support and encouragement in the game of life, and to Carmen and Lyndon Cronen for challenging me to give my best in whatever I do.

I share this little book of cherished memories and experiences I encountered along the many fairways with you, hoping you can enjoy them as much as I have.

May they be an inspiration to you as they have been for me.

# ACKNOWLEDGMENTS

There are many friends who have shared stories that have been extremely valuable for the completion of this book. I appreciate my good friend Joseph F. Girzone, whose support, affirmation, and suggestions continue to challenge me. I am grateful to my friends Christopher Tremblay and Jan Grabinski for proofreading this manuscript. I also want to thank my editor, Fr. Mike Kerrigan, CSP, who has been so gracious and supportive of my ideas, along with the fine staff at Paulist Press for their support, encouragement, and outstanding work in bringing about this book.

# FOREWORD

Games often mimic life, or an aspect of life. Golf is one game that can be easily sublimated, which can in itself be fun. In this delightful little book of reflections, Dorothy K. Ederer cleverly utilizes the jargon and artful strategies of golf to playfully refocus attention on important things in life. The way golfers play the game and the way they react to people and events in the game often reflect the way they react to people and events in their everyday life. Our relationship with God and family and friends are just a few. I know readers will enjoy immensely these poignant and whimsical reflections. They will also find themselves enjoying, perhaps for the first time, praying.

*—Joseph F. Girzone*

# INTRODUCTION

As we reflect on our game, may we be conscious of the Divine Master, who is always there to guide us and help us find the missing links in life.

The prayers and stories for each hole came from the heart of a person whose spirit is energized by the game. Many of the stories were events I witnessed myself, or were told by the persons involved, members of their family, or friends. In parts 3, 4, and 5, the scripture is not the exact wording; rather, I have paraphrased passages to make it more meaningful for all golf lovers.

Hopefully, the other prayers and reflections will lift our minds to God and enhance our concentration.

The "proverbs," "psalms," and "ten commandments" for the golfer remind us of our need to listen to the voice within us as well as that of the Master. Unlike most sports, golf is the one game that has no scapegoats. As we play, we can learn more about ourselves, how we react to our shots, and our final score, as well as what may be going on in our lives. Golf can also reveal to us how we approach life. My "beatitudes" are happy ways of looking at the whimsical coincidences that have occurred to those whose spirit is open to see the Master's humor.

Golf is a humbling sport, as it frustrates while it challenges. It provides delightful opportunities to spend three or four hours not only enjoying the beauty of God's creation, but also having fun walking and talking with friends.

It is my hope that this book can help you focus on your good qualities and learn to accept your handicaps with humor.

# PART ONE

# Reflections As You Walk the Course

# Before Your Game

Divine Master, thank you for offering to be our caddie in life
and allowing our friendship to be based on winter rules.
As we walk the course today, we look forward to your company,
especially as we search in the woods and wander off course.
Each hole is a time to reflect on your presence.
No matter how badly we play, help us get past the red tees.
We will try to face ourselves honestly
and not be discouraged by our handicaps or the hazards that haunt us.

# Psalm 139 for the Golfer

Divine Master, you have watched me and you know me.
You know when I duff and when I divot.
You understand my plays from afar.
My swings and my putts you scrutinize, with all my strokes you
are familiar.
As soon as the ball takes flight, behold, Wise Master, you know
its destination.
Behind me and before me, you help me swing, and rest your hand
upon mine.
Such comfort is too wonderful for me, too lofty for me to comprehend.

Who knows the course of the ball in flight? If it goes into the waters,
    you are there.
If it sinks into the sand trap, you are there. If I wander into barren
    wasteland,
  even there your hand shall guide me, to help me score my best.
Probe me, O God, and know my heart, try me and know my thoughts.
See if my way is crooked, and lead me, if not to a hole in one,
at least to a praiseworthy finish.

4

# HOLE 1

And I will lead the blind in a way that they know not,
in paths that they have not known I will guide them.
I will turn the darkness before them into light,
the rough places into level ground.
These are the things I will do, and I will not forsake them.

Isaiah 42:16

*Divine Master, every now and then we meet extraordinary people. Greg Matthew, a golf pro and owner of the Pine View golf course in Kalamazoo, Michigan, allowed us to take blind students cross-country skiing on his course. He is a role model to so many because of his generous heart.*

Greg became a pro in 1956. He was always a par golfer, but when he lost his sight in 1970 from diabetes, he continued to golf and broke an eighty-six or better every time. In 1980 doctors amputated his right leg. Still he continued to play, happy to break one hundred. In 1996 he had a heart attack while golfing but that, too, didn't stop him.

On December 11, 1998, he was hospitalized for numerous complications. By his bedside were his wife, Jan, his children, Lisa and Tim, and Tim's wife, Lynn. Greg was lying peacefully when all of a sudden he took off his oxygen mask, looked up at his family, and smiled. He saw them for the first time in twenty-eight years. He then asked his wife to kiss him and, after a deep sigh, breathed his last and went home to the Divine Master.

Afterward, his wife told me, "For the first time in twenty-eight years, he could see us. His eyes were no longer covered by a gray film, but were as clear as a blue sky. I know it was a miracle."

*God, you continue to bless us with miracles, most of which pass unnoticed. Shield us from discouragement when tragedy knocks at the door. Give us the courage, as you did Greg, to go on when all seems hopeless.*

# HOLE 2

Pray for us. We are sure that we have a clear conscience and desire to live honorably in every way.

Hebrews 13:18

*O God, it's not easy to be honest when we think we may lose what we aspired to most in life. Bobby Jones showed great integrity in a situation like this.*

In the 1925 U.S. Open, his ball moved when he addressed it. No one else had seen it move, but Bobby did and he had to be honest. He called the penalty on himself, which cost him the championship.

When asked, "Why did you do that?" he responded, "There's only one way to play the game. You might as well praise a man for not robbing a bank as praise him for playing by the rules."

*Divine Master, it cost him the game, but he was admired by millions for his good sportsmanship, even today.*

*Teach me always to be honest with myself and others.*

*Help me to let go of what is not of my doing, and accept what is my fault.*

*Thank you, God, for accepting me and loving me when I make mistakes. Help me to forgive myself.*

*A wise person said, "If you're honest, you'll have the inner peace that so many seek." God, I want that inner peace that comes from being honest.*

# HOLE 3

What the wicked dread will come upon them, but the desire of the righteous will be granted.

Proverbs 10:24

*Divine Master, Lou and Sue Merlo and Mary and Douglas Gregory, wonderful friends, love to tell stories. Here's one you'll enjoy.*

This incident took place in 1915. The president of the Lakeside Country Club, in Tacoma, Washington, Dan McDonald, was playing his first hole there. He had a good drive, but the mashie pitch went wild and struck the side of a cow that had wandered onto the course. Smarting from the blow, the cow kicked and struck the ball just as it hit the ground, sending it onto the green. One putt won the hole. Justice DeWitt M. Evans was there to witness the incident.

*God, we so often see your humor as we live each day. You enjoy surprising us with bizarre situations like this. They bring joy to our weary spirits.*

*What happened to Dan was more than he anticipated.*

*Thank you for the delightful little surprises you send our way. I pray that I may always be grateful, because it is in those unexpected blessings that your presence becomes real.*

# HOLE 4

You must understand this, my beloved: let everyone be quick to listen, slow to speak, slow to anger.

James 1:19

*God, you must cringe every time you hear your name or other words used in vain on the course. Teach us to think before we speak, especially when we find ourselves in situations like the following:*

It was the annual All Saints Regional High School golf outing at Old Brookville Country Club in Long Island, New York. Tom Connolly had a chance to play with home office people from one of the insurance companies he represents. One of the representatives, Bill, a gentle man, was playing six over par at the time. They were on the sixteenth hole. Bill was setting up to take his tee shot; as he raised his club to swing, a beautiful water spaniel appeared out of nowhere, ran up to the ball, grabbed it, and took off. Bill was shocked. As quickly as the dog came, he left, returned the ball back near the tee, then stood off to the side. Bill, upset with the distraction, set up again. The dog repeated the action three more times, but the third time Bill took a different ball and threw it in the direction of another tee nearby. The dog took the cue and dashed off to the other tee, where a man was getting ready to tee off. The dog repeated his act for the other man. Bill quickly made his hit and finished his game. His golfing partners still laugh as they share the incident.

If you are humble and do not take your game too seriously, then you would enjoy playing with someone like this: Joe, with his foursome, was golfing at the Marriott in Bermuda. His ball landed in the fountain at the eighteenth hole. Unperturbed, he was determined to retrieve it. He took off his shoes and socks and stepped in. "Look at all the balls in here. Wow, this is heaven," he yelled to his partner. Then he proceeded to collect them in his shirt.

Their two women companions were so embarrassed that they finished their putts and returned to the clubhouse. Minutes later Joe and his partner arrived. They were like two little kids, showing everyone all the golf balls they had found. People at the clubhouse will never forget Joe.

*Divine Master, grant us the gifts of humility and patience needed when golfing with others. Help us avoid becoming angry or annoyed at the bizarre things that happen on the course. Teach us how to be humble when golfing with someone who doesn't take the game too seriously.*

# HOLE 5

And when you turn to the right or when you turn to the left, your ears shall hear a word behind you, saying, "This is the way; walk in it."

Isaiah 30:21

*Divine Master, my nephew, John Patrick, enjoys telling stories and makes everyone feel welcome just like Stephanie Mansour and her dad Brian, who own the Captain's Club golf course in Grand Blanc, Michigan. They have many interesting stories to tell. Here are a few.*

Freddie Tait, a Scottish amateur, discovered after a shot that his ball had landed inside a small, condensed milk can. Instead of taking an unplayable lie, he just swung at the can. Much to his surprise, it landed on the green. The ball rolled out, stopping right next to the hole.

Byron Nelson, from Texas, was assistant pro at Ridgewood, a fine country club in New Jersey. A member of the club asked him if he could hit a flagpole that was off in the distance. So Byron took a one iron and aimed. The ball flew through the air and, to everyone's surprise, hit the pole. Years later he won the 1942 Masters against Ben Hogan.

*O God, sometimes we accomplish the unexplainable and shock ourselves. In these moments of inconceivable events I become more aware of your presence in my life.*

*Everything is a gift from you. Teach me to rejoice in the present moment, and not take anything for granted.*

# HOLE 6

But now thus says the LORD, he who created you, O Jacob, he who formed you, O Israel: Do not fear, for I have redeemed you; I have called you by name, you are mine.

Isaiah 43:1

*Divine Master, each of us was created for a special purpose, and no matter what handicaps we may have, you will achieve your plan through us if we are willing to let go and trust. These two men's disability did not stop them from allowing your plan to be accomplished.*

In 1954 Ed Furgol, with his crippled arm, won the U.S. Open.

In 1998 Casey Martin, who has a rare disease that would eventually cause him to lose his leg, fought the golf establishment and won the right to play golf in the PGA tournaments and ride in a golf cart. Today he competes against the world's best golfers on the PGA Tour, even though he has a crippled leg.

*God, it is so difficult to believe we can achieve things we really want when we have a disability. These two men have inspired many to pursue a dream, even when all the odds were against them. If we can trust and put our faith in you, anything can happen.*

# HOLE 7

And why do you worry about clothing? Consider the lilies of the field, how they grow; they neither toil nor spin.

Matthew 6:28

*Divine Master, we know you'll be there to guide us no matter how we appear to others.*

I had to laugh when someone shared this story with me: Margaret Abbott, an American, was visiting Paris as the 1900 Olympic Games were about to begin. She was not an official U.S. athlete, but she was allowed to enter the women's golf competition. Not having proper attire, she golfed in high-heel shoes and a short skirt. She was the first woman to win an Olympic gold medal.

*O God, we admire Margaret for accepting a challenge and not being afraid of possible ridicule. Help us not to be concerned about what others think or how we look, but to be secure in who we are.*

*Every day we face circumstances that are challenging; we can either ignore or embrace them. But when we respond to the unthinkable, our life can become a wonderful adventure!*

# HOLE 8

And let the peace of Christ rule in your hearts, to which indeed you were called in the one body. And be thankful.

Colossians 3:15

*Divine Master, sometimes you bless us with those unexpected blessings, and a simple "thank you" seems empty. These two men were thrilled at what happened to them.*

In Santa Ana, California, during a 1977 round at the River View golf course, Dean Colbert, with a little nudge from his brother, made a hole in one at the ninth hole. Dean hit the ball first and it landed inches from the cup. His brother, Ken, followed with a drive that looked just like his brother's. Ken's ball nudged Dean's into the cup. Match-play rules at the time stipulated a golfer had a choice—replace the ball in its original lie or accept its new position. Well, we all know that Dean didn't have to think twice. He accepted the ace graciously and thanked the Master.

During the Depression, in 1930, in order to keep the course open, the city of Portland, Oregon, offered lifetime memberships at any of the municipal courses for one hundred dollars. They sold two hundred life passes. Little did they know that Lou Rose, who bought a life pass, would still be using it today. "There are a couple of others still alive, but he is the only one still playing at the Eastmoreland golf course," said Clark Pumpston, the golf pro.

> *Divine Master, there are so many little things that happen to us each day that we are grateful for. Inspire us to take time to give thanks for the many blessings that come our way.*

# HOLE 9

...to teach shrewdness to the simple, knowledge and prudence to the young—
let the wise also hear and gain in learning, and the discerning acquire skill.

Proverbs 1:4–5

*Divine Master, when we meet a generous person, we can't help but wish
we were more giving. Often the expression of goodwill means more to the
person than the help we actually give. But in this situation, Lee Trevino's
help was a blessing to those desperately in need.*

In 1971 Lee Trevino won the British Open at Royal Birkdale. The people
running the tournament told him that it was a tradition for the champion to
give a portion of his check to the local Catholic orphanage. He agreed to give
fifteen hundred dollars, but on one condition: the nuns from the orphanage
had to come and have a glass of champagne with him at the nearby Kingway
Casino. Naturally the sisters agreed, even though they had never been in the
casino or had ever had a drink. Lee was so touched by it all that he auctioned
off the clubs he used to win the Open and donated the proceeds, another fifteen hundred dollars, to the kids at the orphanage.

*O God, what a glorious day for the sisters! Lee's generosity won their hearts. The children at the orphanage realized that not only would their physical needs be taken care of, but also that they were loved. That made a difference.*

# HOLE 10

When you pass through the waters, I will be with you; and through the rivers, they shall not overwhelm you; when you walk through fire you shall not be burned, and the flame shall not consume you.

Isaiah 43:2

*God, whenever there is water along the course, my ball is sure to find it.*

In 1988 I was golfing with Jackie Sanders and Fr. John Grathwohl when my ball plunged into a pond off the first green at the Elks Club in Kalamazoo.

Jackie, a young college student, yelled, "I'll get it!" She bent over to retrieve the ball, her feet slipped, and she plunged headfirst into the muddy waters.

Fr. John laughed so hard he fell to the ground. "I've never seen anything like this!" he said. Giggling, I said to Jackie, "Are you all right?"

Seconds later, Jackie popped out of the water, her body draped in weeds and muck, and held the ball in the air, laughing, "I got it! I got it!"

That year she received a ball retriever for graduation.

*God, your humor shows in many little ways. As Jackie, covered with mud and weeds, could laugh at herself as she held the ball high, may we always see humor in stressful times. Life is meant to be embraced, enjoyed, and celebrated!*

# HOLE 11

In this you rejoice, even if now for a little while you have had to suffer various trials.

1 Peter 1:6

*Divine Master, my expectations are high, and I become discouraged when I don't do as well as I think I should. Sometimes I get so caught up with achievement that I forget not only the rules but the role that you play in my success.*

In the 1959 Chicago Open, Billy Casper hit his tee shot into the middle of a thick mulberry bush at the eleventh hole. He was not aware that he could have taken a free drop. It took him ten strokes to free the ball. He lost the Open by three strokes.

*Wise Master, how many times have I been unaware of rules or forgotten to read instructions because of the excitement of the moment? It is difficult to give up, especially when you believe you can do it. We can all identify with Billy in his determination to accomplish what he set out to do. Knowing the rules of the game can help us avoid these frustrating moments.*

*Help me to continue to struggle when things get rough and to realize you are there to help me in times of need. I need your grace to help me reflect on your presence in tough situations.*

# HOLE 12

[Love] does not rejoice in wrongdoing, but rejoices in the truth. It bears all things, believes all things, hopes all things, endures all things.

1 Corinthians 13:6-7

*Divine Master, love is relentless. It calls us to accept challenges when we are not always sure of the outcome, as in this situation with Arnold Palmer.*

Arnie was just out of the Coast Guard, but already had a great reputation as an amateur golfer. He wanted to get married, but he didn't have enough money to buy Winnie an engagement ring.

Some of his friends said they would pay him one hundred dollars for every stroke he made under par seventy-two at the Pine Valley course in Clementon, New Jersey. But, for every stroke over eighty, he would have to pay *them* one hundred dollars. Arnie scored a sixty-eight. Well, you know the rest. He was so excited that he went out and bought her the ring, and they lived happily ever after.

*Divine Master, love like that is a God-given love to be celebrated. To love another is to make God's love visible to the world. We come alive when we know we are loved and accepted for who we are. We then find ourselves looking at others with new eyes, and with kinder and more forgiving hearts.*

*O God, teach me to love as you do. As I learn to give more of myself, I learn how to love more unselfishly. I pray that all my relationships will come alive through your spirit.*

# HOLE 13

The light of the eyes rejoices the heart, and good news refreshes the body.

Proverbs 15:30

*God, so many people are gifted in golf, including many young people like the following.*

Tiger Woods has been blessed with an incredible gift for golf. He swung his first golf club when he was six months old. At two he was matching putts with Bob Hope on *The Mike Douglas Show*. At three, he played his first round of golf and shot a forty-eight for nine holes. Some people who've been playing for years get excited when they get a score like that for nine holes. He continues to soar on the courses.

A twenty-five-year-old South Korean woman, Se Ri Pak, won the United States Women's Open and the Jamie Farr Kroger Classic. She shot a round of sixty-one, the lowest score ever in the Ladies Professional Golf Association, and finished twenty-three under par. Her role model is Nancy Lopez, who has won a total of forty-eight tournaments in her career. She admires Nancy for being a fantastic golfer and for her smile and happy spirit.

*God, we all have gifts and talents, but encouragement, a person's smile, and positive attitude can bring joy to the human heart. Bringing joy and inspiration to others is also a great gift. People are searching for acceptance and love, and a smile tells a lonely person that someone cares. We all want to make a difference, but often we do not know how. Sometimes it takes only a word of encouragement to one who is gifted and talented. To acknowledge and support others can give them the hope needed to continue. For some that's all it takes.*

# HOLE 14

He said to them, "Because of your little faith. For truly I tell you, if you have faith the size of a mustard seed, you will say to this mountain, 'Move from here to there,' and it will move; and nothing will be impossible for you."

Matthew 17:20

*Divine Master, after hearing this story, I found myself singing one of Marty Haugen's songs, "We Walk by Faith."*

Sister Lisa Marie's dad, Chuck Lazio, a golfer since he was sixteen, went legally blind from macular degeneration in 1980. His six daughters (four are nuns, two are golfers) weren't sure if he'd want to golf again. "I may be blind, but I can't stop living," he said. "I'm still going to play golf."

He continued to play and got a hole in one five times—one at the Gulf Gate course and four at the Village Green, in Sarasota, Florida. At eighty-seven he suffered a stroke on the golf course. Even after his retirement he continued to inspire others, especially his grandson, a golfer and pilot, not to give up no matter what obstacles come their way.

*Divine Master, Chuck walked by faith, not by sight.*
   *Thank you for your presence in people like him, who allow your love and goodness to radiate.*

*Thank you for those who have shown compassion and hope during weary and bleak moments.*

*Thank you for assuring us that you are with us when we are lonely and lost.*

*Thank you for teaching us patience as we continue to search for our way in life.*

# HOLE 15

Give her a share in the fruit of her hands, and let her works praise her in the city gates.

Proverbs 31:31

*Divine Master, a passage in the Book of Proverbs describes the ideal woman: "She makes linen garments and sells them, and supplies the merchants with sashes. She is clothed with strength and dignity; she can laugh at the days to come. She speaks with wisdom, and faithful instruction is on her tongue."*

In ages past, that was the ideal woman. Consider the following as an ideal woman for our time. She started golfing at twenty-one, and soon became an assistant pro. She was the Ladies Professional Golf Association (LPGA) tournament director and gained a lifetime membership in the LPGA teaching division. She was an FAA certified flight and ground school instructor, and owned ten different planes. She received an impressive award from Foothill College, in Los Altos Hills, California, where she taught aviation for eighteen years. She was elected to the International Women's Sports Hall of Fame. At seventy-eight she took part in her own tournament for single professional women, which she sponsored for twenty-four years. She has published three books—two on golf and one on cooking. She is a skilled artist who has done exquisite drawings of LPGA and Hollywood notables, and has played the cello since age twelve. She is a golfer, historian, teacher, writer, artist, and musician. Betty Hicks has earned a place in our hearts and in the history of golf. She surely is a model woman for our times.

*Divine Master, we are grateful to you for the people who love us and challenge us to new and exciting adventures. Enlighten us to know our gifts and talents and teach us how to overcome the fear of sharing them.*

# HOLE 16

Therefore, since we are surrounded by so great a cloud of witnesses, let us also lay aside every weight and the sin that clings so closely, and let us run with perseverance the race that is set before us.

Hebrews 12:1

*Divine Master, the following people were determined never to abandon their dreams. With Your constant help they succeeded wonderfully.*

Babe Zaharias was an American athlete who excelled in many sports. She won a place on the All-American women's basketball team and three national records in track and field events. She set records for the javelin throw and the eighty-meter hurdle. She won two gold medals and a silver in the Olympics. She then decided to take up golf, and from 1936 to 1954 won the British and U.S. Women's Amateur, four world championships, and three U.S. Women's Opens before she died from cancer. She was one of the founding members of the LPGA. She has been considered by many one of the most outstanding women athletes of the twentieth century.

Nancy Lopez is easily the greatest woman golfer of our time. At her peak, she could drive the ball an average of 265 yards. She has won forty-eight tournaments, including every major except the Open. She has recently accepted the United States Golf Association's Bob Jones Award, the most prestigious award in golf. She is one of only nine to receive it. Nancy is the only member of the Hall of Fame to get there while raising a family. She is the first woman to create and launch clubs specifically designed under her name.

Jack Nicklaus, an outstanding golfer and a legend of our time, has been a great inspiration to the younger generation. Often it is difficult for people who have been pros in any particular field to watch the younger generation rise to fame. What is so nice about Jack is that he rejoices when younger golfers succeed, as long as they are good role models for our young people. It has always been important in his golf and in his life.

Don Pooley, who aced the 192-yard seventeenth hole at the Hertz Bay Classic in Orlando, Florida, would never give up. The hole in one gave him a half-million-dollar bonus, which has been known as the largest single-hole prize in golf history.

*Divine Master, these people wouldn't give up on their dream. Their determination and dedication brought them where they are today.*

*May we place our trust in you and avoid any anxiety or worry as we walk joyfully with you down the fairway of life. Grant us the insight to recognize the blessings that come our way.*

# HOLE 17

Commit your work to the LORD, and your plans will be established.

Proverbs 16:3

*Divine Master, you inspired the following people to share their love for those suffering from a disability. It is incredible how quickly we recover when we are loved and affirmed.*

Bev Regan and Laura Giandomenico, therapeutic recreation specialists, discovered how lessons about balance and range of motion are surprisingly similar to the lessons golf professionals teach. They contacted Mike Olizarevitch, a golf pro at the city-owned Fanshawe Golf and Country Club, in London, Ontario, which has two Regulation Nine courses for the handicapped. It is the only golf course he knows of in North America that is designed specifically for the physically challenged. The holes are fifty to one hundred and fifty yards long and entirely wheelchair accessible.

Mike enlisted two fellow pros, Fred Kern and Andy Shaw, also unpaid volunteers, to help. Twenty clinics have proven successful by combining rehabilitation efforts with golf techniques. Some of the participants could make shots and putts even if they were amputees, spinal-cord injured, or otherwise wheelchair bound.

Mike said, "We are making a difference. I worked with a stroke patient, and after six weeks of therapy he was playing the course. It's so rewarding, instilling confidence and seeing them progress so fast. One of my greatest joys is seeing the smiles on their faces. I tell them, 'If you can dream it, you can do it.' We hold special events here and are opening the course this year for children ages three to nine, so they can start playing."

> *Divine Master, it is difficult to know what you have in mind for each of us. When we use our gifts to encourage others to become better, it's amazing the effect it has on us. Standing by a dreamer's side and working with him as he takes his first steps is one of the most rewarding experiences.*
>     *Encourage us to respond to the spirit within*
>     *so we can bring life to those who may be losing hope.*

# HOLE 18

Blessed is anyone who endures temptation. Such a one has stood the test and will receive the crown of life that the Lord has promised to those who love him.

James 1:12

*Divine Master, it is a miracle how Ben Hogan and his wife survived a nearly fatal auto accident.*

While Ben was bending over to save his wife's life, his left leg was crushed, his ankle fractured, and his pelvis and left collarbone broken. Because of head injuries, he was visually impaired. Complications set in, blood clots in his left leg migrated to his lungs, and the doctors didn't think he would live. Emergency surgery saved his life, but he would always have pain in his legs.

After spending two months in the hospital, it was seven months before he could hit a golf ball again. Sixteen months later he entered the U.S. Open. He was in so much pain that he could hardly stand up after each swing. He almost quit because he didn't think he could walk the final eighteen holes, but he continued to wrap his legs and stayed to finish. Ben was able to stand the test and come back and win six times in the most prestigious golf tournaments in the world: three U.S. Opens, two Masters, and a British Open.

*Divine Healer, I admire Ben's determination and courage to continue to go on when all seemed hopeless. His determination and dedication are an inspiration.*

*Changes in our life are very difficult to accept at times. Shield me from any harm and help me to be patient with myself as I find my way in this world.*

# HOLE 19

Rejoice in the Lord always; again I will say, Rejoice.

Philippians 4:4

*Divine Master, finishing our game we approach the nineteenth hole with anticipation. This reminds me of the final nineteenth hole of life as we arrive at your banquet, where the joy and celebration will be out of this world.*

Christopher Tremblay rejoiced with me when I shared with him this story, since he worked with Lowell Rinker for years. As we approached the nineteenth hole one day, we had great reason to celebrate. It was a beautiful sunny day in June at the Ridgeview Golf Course in Kalamazoo. Kathy and Lowell Rinker, Jackie and Gary Shuk, and I had just finished a fun afternoon of golf. At the beginning, Lowell, as usual, had hassled the women about the unfairness of the distance between the women's and men's tee. As we approached the tenth tee, Lowell was still going on. "You girls got it made—twenty yards before you even shoot."

"We're just trying to follow the rules, but if that's the way you feel, I'll play from the men's tee," I said.

He laughed. "This should be interesting," he said.

I took my five wood (which Lowell had made for me) and a Slazenger ball (from a friend, Jim Merna). Gary threw me a red tee, saying, "Here, you'll need all the help you can get."

Giggling, I tried to compose myself. I swung and the ball sailed off into the air. I didn't even bother looking, but walked over to put my club into the bag.

Gary yelled, "It went in! It went in! She got a hole in one."

Lowell laughed. "No way, you've got to be joking."

"Honest, I saw it go in!" said Gary.

Thinking they were making fun, I ignored them and got in my cart and waited for Jackie and Kathy to tee off.

As we all proceeded up the fairway, Lowell still joked about the disappearing ball until we reached the green. I stood there, stunned. "It did go in, it did go in!" I shouted.

"I told you it did," Gary said in desperation.

"Well, Dort, I have to take the ball," Jackie said.

"No way, that ball brought me luck."

"But that's the rule. The ball has to be retired," she insisted.

Reluctantly, I gave her the ball.

Then Lowell started in again. "Now listen, Sis, you really didn't have much to do with this, you know."

"What do you mean by that?" I said.

"Well, I made you the club, Jim gave you the Slazenger ball, and Gary gave you the tee. And everybody knows you don't get a hole in one without help from above. God's just playing tricks and you merely went along for the ride. Besides, I can't take any more of this, so now get back to the woman's tee where you belong."

We all chuckled and played on.

Tom Biber, the owner of the course, was in the clubhouse at the time and saw all the commotion on the green. When we finished the game and went inside, he asked what had happened. We told him the story.

Lowell continued his hassling. "Who ever gets a hole in one is supposed to buy a round of drinks," he said.

The girls all came to my defense and insisted that Lowell buy the drinks. And in his customary generous manner, he agreed and treated us to a round of lemonade. And the celebration began!

*Divine Master, we thank you for the peak experiences in our lives. It is in moments like these that we feel a profound sense of your personal love. These highs sustain us and encourage us to continue. Thank you for thrilling experiences.*

Three months later, Jackie had the ball mounted on a beautiful plaque that read:

ON THE 28TH DAY OF JUNE 1994
DOROTHY K. EDERER
APPROACHED THE 10TH HOLE AT
RIDGEVIEW GOLF COURSE.
SHE TOOK A 5 WOOD OUT OF HER BAG
AND SMACKED THIS VERY BALL 155 YARDS.
AT 2:23 P.M. IT WAS DECLARED:
A HOLE IN ONE.
SOME SAY IT WAS "DIVINE INTERVENTION."

PART TWO

# Prayers and Reflections for the Golfer

# Opening Prayer

Wise Master, we enter your presence to ask your forgiveness
for the times we failed to stay on course.

We have come upon rough times; we have fallen into sandy traps
and strayed into barren wasteland and murky waters,
    all because of our handicap.

Forgive us, God.
Help us to avoid the traps of feeling that we must always play a perfect
        game,
always on par, or of being depressed when our game is below expectations.
We are often tempted to give up when we go off course and in the rough,
failing to trust you'll guide us back into play.

As we continue on the way, we still hook and slice rather than follow the
        straight way.
We are fearful of what lies ahead, especially when we approach a dogleg.
In time we will learn to trust you.

Help us to be aware of the divots we make in life,
and how often we fail to replace them, hoping no one will notice.

As we continually start anew, give us the grace to plant our feet firmly on
the ground,
face the right direction, and steady with our heads down and still, swing
slow.

May we concentrate on following through as we drive forward with
renewed intent.
Give us strength to face ourselves honestly and not be discouraged by our
handicap.
May we have the assurance that, although we did not make par, or hit a
hole in one,
you will still welcome us into the clubhouse, where all struggling golfers,
even duffers,
are welcome to your party at the nineteenth hole.

## Words of Encouragement

As the Divine Master's chosen people, holy and dearly loved,
clothe yourselves with compassion, kindness, humility, gentleness, and
patience.
Bear with each other and forgive whatever grievances you may have against
one another.
Forgive as God forgave you.
And over all these virtues put on love, which binds them all together in
perfect unity.

Let the peace of the Divine Master rule in your hearts, since as members of
   one body
you were called to peace. And be thankful.

Let the word of the Divine Master dwell in you richly as you teach and
   admonish one another
with all wisdom, and as you sing psalms and spiritual songs with gratitude
   in your hearts
to the Divine Master.

And whatever you do, whether in word or deed, do it all in the name of the
   Holy One,
giving thanks to the Divine Master through him.

—adapted from Colossians 3:12–17

# Reflections

## HANDICAP

*Based on our average score*

Whatever our handicap, it should never be an excuse for doing less than our best. May we not be discouraged by our handicaps. They often provide the push we need to accomplish heroic undertakings, which will affect the lives of others significantly.

*Divine Master, I pray that I can accept my handicap and not let it distract me.*

*Restore in me faith to believe in myself again.*
*Surround me with your love and grace.*
*Continue to give me the courage and desire to love and serve others the*
*way you do.*

## TEE

*Things we set ourselves up for*

### RIDICULE AND PRAISE

We each long for praise in things we do well, regardless of the situation or circumstance. We cannot ignore the need for affirmation and encouragement. Each time we are praised for something we've done well, most often we become better. We often become what people expect of us.

The same is true of ridicule. It can drag us down and undermine our confidence. Sometimes we may even question our value as a person. So often when we are mean and nasty, it is because we are hurting. Knowing we are loved and accepted for who we are makes a great difference.

Our game can be seriously affected if we've had an argument with someone we value, or are worried about something that's happening in our life. Stay focused on the present moment and concentrate and you will play much better.

### BLAME OR SHAME

Shame is feeling bad about who we are. It develops out of our perception of what others think of us. So often when we are shamed, we blame others because we are disappointed in ourselves. There is a sense of shame that happens to us when we blame others, mostly because we haven't been able to accept responsibility for our actions. But in time we will learn, grow, and become the person we want to be. We can overcome our shame if we recognize our mistakes and work to conquer them.

*Divine Master, as I open my heart to your love,*
*may I praise and affirm my partner*
*and see the goodness that stems from a right relationship with you.*
*Heal me of any painful memories, and help me to avoid hurting others*
*when I've been betrayed.*
*May I anticipate with joy what you have in store for me*
*as I journey down the fairway to healing.*

## DOGLEG

*A major turn in our path*

- Sicknesses
- Loss of a Job
- Loss of a Loved One

Our sicknesses and losses weigh heavily on our minds and hearts, but we learn something from each of them. Some losses may seem unbearable. Usually people who have suffered most are the ones who are the most compassionate. When we lose a job or a loved one, it takes time and patience to adjust. The healing process begins gradually as we learn to let go. We never know what lies ahead, but if we put our trust in God, it makes sickness and loss a little easier to accept.

*Divine Master, I welcome your presence in every situation I will face today.*
*May those who cross my path experience your joy and love.*
*Encourage me to accept whatever losses may come my way.*

## HOOKS AND SLICES

Depending on our aim, we may be hitting some good shots, but in the wrong direction. The Master will allow us to start fresh at any point in our life. It is never too late to get our life back on course, no matter what may have thrown us off course.

*Divine Master, sometimes we feel we're aiming right,*
*but after a few strokes our sights are misdirected.*
*Forgive me for the times I've strayed from you.*
*Increase my sensitivity to others as I walk through life.*

## SAND TRAPS

*Things in life difficult to overcome*

### PERFECTIONISM

The game of golf is a game of accepting failure; of accepting imperfection; of realizing that the perfect game has never been played, never will be played, or ever could be played. (Author unknown)

God doesn't expect us to be perfect, only to strive for it. God is patient with our mistakes. God may not like some of the things we do, but God is never disappointed in who we are, as long as we are trying and doing our best. If we are expecting ourselves to be perfect, we will only become anxious. In striving for perfection, it is important that we love ourselves as we are, and accept our strengths and weaknesses as we become aware of them. Becoming aware of our weaknesses can be uncomfortable at first, but it is the first step in taking giant strides to becoming more loving and forgiving.

## UNREALISTIC EXPECTATIONS

We often expect more of ourselves than we do of others. It's good to set goals, but make them realistic and attainable. We have to be careful not to expect more from ourselves than we are capable of. It can dampen our spirit. God loves us the way we are. We can still love ourselves as we are and work hard for change.

## DECEIT

When someone is not honest, it usually springs from the fear of being rejected. We may hold back the truth or something important, thinking it will not harm the relationship, but it does not always help us or others. Deceit has often destroyed marriages, lost jobs, and soured relationships. Bertha Conde expressed it so well when she said, "Every friendship that lasts is built of certain durable materials. The first of these is truthfulness. If I can look into the eyes of my friend and always speak out the truthful thought and feeling with the simplicity of a little child, there will be a real friendship between us." I am convinced that a relationship built on truthfulness has more chances of surviving than one that is not. We all desire to be loved and accepted. It is much easier to accept and forgive a person who is humble enough to speak the truth to us, even when it hurts. We will be respected more because of our honesty. We may fail to realize we are deceiving others by not counting all our strokes, but what we are really doing is hurting ourselves.

## HYPOCRISY

Do we blame others for something we ourselves do? For example, an individual is upset because his partner failed to count a stroke when he retrieved his ball from the woods and placed it on the fairway. That same person turns around and moves his ball away from a tree because it was impossible to hit, but refused to count it as a stroke. Most of the time, we become angry or upset when we see traits in others we ourselves possess.

What sand traps have slowed you down spiritually?

*Divine Master, often I feel I have to do everything perfectly to receive your love,*
*but I know you will always love me, even when I don't always do my best.*
*I will continue to forgive and love myself as I work toward changing those things*
*that make me the person you would like me to be.*
*I will strive always to be honest with myself and others as I speak the truth,*
*even if no one listens, even if no one understands why.*
*As I become aware of my weaknesses,*
*may I also be more aware of your eternal love for me.*

## OUT OF BOUNDS

Success in life or in golf depends upon how concentrated our focus is. Sometimes we act quickly, fail to concentrate, and end up off course or in rough places.

*Divine Master, I recognize the times I have strayed from you.*
*Forgive me for the pain I have caused others because of my weaknesses.*
*May I return, through your grace and love, to live my life on the path of*
*goodness?*
*Thank you for your mercy. Help me focus and concentrate on what I am*
*doing in life.*

### PAINFUL RELATIONSHIPS

We may find ourselves denying that the relationship we are in is not healthy for either of us. We do it as a way of protecting ourselves. We refuse to acknowledge the reality until we feel prepared to cope with the situation. Some of us need time to prepare ourselves and figure out how we will cope. People can scream the truth, but unless we are ready to listen, we may not make a wise choice.

In golf, it is extremely difficult to concentrate on the game if someone is constantly giving suggestions or correcting a play. It's not so much what one may be saying, but how it is said. Some people fight more on a golf course than anywhere else.

## DEPRESSION

We may be depressed for a number of reasons:

1. When we fail to obtain that which we seek.
2. When we can't live up to our expectations.
3. When another has what we want.
4. When we compare ourselves to others.

We want to do our best. A bad shot or a high score can spoil our day. We need to learn not to take the game so seriously. Golf is a sport to be enjoyed. We do better when we are relaxed.

## REJECTION BY OTHERS

If we expect everyone to love us, we will never be happy. No matter how good we are, or how famous we are, all of us at some time in our lives have experienced rejection. Even the Divine Master was rejected. We can't expect better for ourselves.

## INJUSTICES (EITHER TO YOU OR SOMEONE YOU LOVE)

Whenever we find ourselves angry or irritated with someone, it may not be the person but something about ourselves that bothers us. So often we hurt others because we are hurting.

We don't like to see injustice in a sport. Being human, we'll make mistakes, stumble, and fall along the fairway of life, but it's how we pick ourselves up and go on that is important to the Master.

## WATER HOLES

*Situations difficult to get out of*

How have you responded to the water holes in your life? Reflect on these words of Lee Trevino: There are two things you can do with your head down: play golf and pray.

> *Divine Master, sometimes I fail to respond lovingly to the water holes in my life.*
> *Help me to listen as I make wise choices on how to live my life more for you.*
> *Relationships can be painful, but when you are the center of them, those painful and stressful times become easier.*

## DRIVER OR PUTTER?

*Is our drive to always succeed or can we putt along, taking what life gives us?*

We live in a world where success sometimes is viewed as more important than family or friends. We may spend more time getting ahead and less time developing friendships and bonding with our family. Or we can trust the Master, who has a hand in it all, and accept what comes our way as part of the game.

> *Divine Master, may I never let success or fame be my goal,*
> *but strive always to be in a right relationship with you as I putt along through life.*

# A MULLIGAN

*Thank God for the second chances in life*

God always gives us second chances. We are given the right to be human, to be weak, to stumble and fall, but as long as we continue to reach out and forgive not only those who hurt us, but also ourselves, we are pleasing in the Master's eyes. When we find it in our heart to forgive and realize that what someone did to us was a result of weakness, imperfection, and impatience, then we free ourselves. As long as we harbor anger and resentment, we will never be free. Our prayer life will lack power, our jobs and relationships will be affected, and our health will suffer. We all want a second chance; let's pray we will give it to others.

*Divine Master, often you have given me second chances.*
*Forgive me for the times I've refused to give others the same.*
*Help me to be sensitive to others who are hurting.*
*Increase my vision to see the pain and brokenness in others.*
*Keep me meek in offering my opinion.*
*Teach me how to forgive myself when I offend someone.*
*Transform me into the person I am to become.*

# Closing Prayer

Wise Master, in the game of life
You know that though most of us are duffers, we all aspire to be champions.

Help us, we pray, to be grateful for the course,
including both the fairways and the rough.
Thank you for those who have made it possible for us to tee off.
Thank you for the thrill of a solid, soaring drive,
the challenge of the dogleg,
the trial of the trap,
the discipline of the water hazard,
and the beauty of a cloudless sky.

Thank you, God, our Master and Pro, who shows us how to get the right
grip on life,
to slow down our back swing,
to correct our crazy hooks and slices,
to keep our heads down in humility,
and to follow through in self-control.

Teach us also to be good sports who will accept the rub of the green,
the penalty for wandering out of bounds,
the reality of lost balls, the relevancy of par,
and the dangers of the nineteenth hole.

And when our last putt has dropped into the cup,
and the light of our last day has faded into darkness,
though our trophies be few, our handicap still too high,
and, for most of us, the hole in one still only a dream,
may we be able to turn in to you,

our tournament director at the great clubhouse,
an honest scorecard.
Amen.

—Author unknown. Adapted by Dorothy K. Ederer

PART THREE

# Readings
# Adapted from the
# Old Testament

# Proverbs 2:1–15, 20–21

For those of you who play on my fairways and take my words to heart,
whose numbers are transparent and show no trace of smudges,
who follow precisely the rules of my fairways,
I will send you wisdom, and she will guide you all along the way.
Whatever direction you take, whatever force or energy you need,
wisdom will be there to assure you.
When you get lost in deep grass, or in dark and dangerous, woody areas,
she will be by your side. She will hold you by the hand, showing you
    the clubs
you need as she leads you through the darkness.

If you run into deep valleys or traps along the way,
wisdom will be there to show you the angles and guide your hand.
When you are in a sand trap together, she will make you laugh.
Take the time to enjoy her playful humor
as she shows you yet another side of God.

For the Divine Master is the father of wisdom,
and through her, he shows his masterful knowledge of the twists and turns
on the fairways and guides us through shallow and deep waters along
    the way.

Remember, imperfect vision, bad math, and discounted figures
can strip the game of fun and cause congenial comrades
to look askance and wonder.

The Divine Master reserves his special awards for the honest and the
fun-loving.
Through his wisdom, he gives his best advice to those whose vision is
straight,
whose heart is clear. Because he is true to himself and others, he earns the
trust of all his comrades.
He is the first they call for another match.

When wisdom comes into your heart, she does not leave you.
She is by your side, not only in your golf game
but in the bigger game of life.
She is your true friend and lover, never to abandon you
or leave you alone.
For she trusts your honesty and clean heart,
as well as your generous spirit of gratitude.
Because your honesty and simplicity make
you vulnerable, she will guide you with her cautious
wisdom and prudent guidance. You will never have to
fear the fox or the crawling things along the way.
And in the end, she will be proud to add her name to yours as you
turn in your scorecard to the Divine Master.

# Proverbs 3:1-8

No long, heavy instructions do I give my friends
as you begin to play along my fairway.
Instead I share the good news with you
to increase your enjoyment of the game.
If you treasure my guidance, you will find that I know
every twist and turn along your way. It may surprise you that
in following my guidance you have avoided many traps and tricky bunkers.
In the end, you will enjoy the game immensely and find that
I am a quiet partner, whose presence brings you peace
and pleasure along the way.
By following my gentle suggestions, you will find yourself
more accomplished in your game than you would have imagined.
Include me in every game you play and you will know
that I am the best friend you could ever have.

# Proverbs 3:13–18

Blessed are the golfers who have discovered wisdom in playing the game.
They have played for fun with humorous humility,
showing no haughty airs or impatience with others
with less expertise.
They have found that enjoyment and wisdom are more important than
      winning.
For it is far better to enjoy your friends than to triumph over them.
You will then always win even when you lose.
For wisdom's values are different from ours.
She often sees success where we see failure.
In pursuing our goals, she often sees greater benefits for us
when we fail to attain what we had hoped for.
Her ways are filled with delight, her paths all lead to contentment.
She helps us work on the playful mystery behind the game,
and encourages us to look within ourselves for its hidden rewards.
For it is wisdom who will help you discern decisions
that will give you life, and in clinging to her,
she will assure you a happy life!

# Ecclesiastes 3:1–8

There is a season for golf and a time for every sport under the heavens.

A time for keeping silent as another golfer tees off.

A time for cheering, when one's ball rolls in for a hole in one.

A time for searching for golf balls in the water or off the fairway.

A time for supporting one another, when the ball lands in the middle of the fairway.

A time for tears, when you miss the putt that cost you the game.

A time for laughing as one's ball goes into the lake and hits a beaver.

A time for mourning, when another player misses the putt that would have given him a birdie.

A time for dancing, when your team wins the championship!

A time for throwing golf balls back when they don't belong to you.

A time for gathering golf balls when they go in between the trees.

A time for encouraging people, to play their best and be themselves.

A time for forgiving ourselves, when we don't get the score we wanted.

A time for reconciliation with those who have hurt us by sarcastic comments while golfing.

A time for landing in the sand trap, and getting out with one stroke.

A time for keeping an honest score card.

A time for discarding our beatup golf balls.

A time for compliments, when others get a birdie or a hole in one.

A time for loving and honoring the creator of the fairways and this wonderful game!

# The Ten Commandments for the Golfer

1. The Divine Master will always be number one, thy family second, and golf third.
2. God's name will be used only to praise.
3. Every day will be holy, with the Master as thy partner.
4. Thou shall not pick up golf balls while they are still rolling.
5. Thou shall not try to kill the ball; an easy stroke will take it farther.
6. Thou shall not steal tees or balls from thy partner's golf bag.
7. Thou shall count all thy strokes.
8. Thou shall witness thy partner's birdie, which landed one inch from the hole.
9. Thou shall not covet thy partner's score.
10. Thou shall not covet thy neighbor's golf sweaters.

# PART FOUR

# Psalms
# for the Golfer

## Psalm 1: True Happiness

Happy the one who follows not the counsel of beginners, nor looks down
upon the lowly, nor speaks while others take careful aim, but delights when
someone pars, or even better, makes a birdie, and is not envious when
    someone aces or plays a perfect game.
Such a person is like an eagle in the air that soars above the less thoughtful
and thrives in difficult situations; he is consistent on whatever course
    he plays.
Even when he loses, he wins

## Psalm 16:7–11: Prayer Against Opponents

I bless my God, my Guide, who counsels me; even in a hazard my heart
    exalts you.
I place the ball before me; with you at my right, I shall not go astray.
My heart is glad, my spirit rejoices, my body too relaxes in confidence.
Because you will not allow the ball to go into strange or desolate places,
nor will you allow a brand new ball to sink in muddy waters.
You show me the sure way home along a crooked fairway,
and fullness of joy when I arrive.
You delight when on a rare occasion my ball strikes the pin and
falls gently into the hole.

# Psalm 18:2–4, 7: Thanksgiving for Help and Victory

I love you, my Guide; you are my strength and comfort.
You give me confidence as I choose the appropriate instrument for the
    fairway stroke.
I praise you, God, for you protect me from the hazards in life.
In my distress I so often called upon you.
How often you came to assist me
when I drifted into four-foot-high bunkers.
From a distance you knew my need
and immediately came to my aid. You are always by my side to guide and
    uphold me.
I love You, O God, my Counsel and Guide.

# Psalm 23: The Lord Is My Guide

The Lord is my guide, I shall not worry.
In verdant courses he sets my feet.
From dangerous waters he leads me, refreshing my spirit.
He guides me on straight paths for a clearer aim.
Even though at times I end up in rough places,
I have no fears, for the gentle Master is there to help me.
With my woods and irons, I progress from tee to greens with hope and
    exultation.

You created the beautiful landscape before me to be enjoyed with all my
friends.
You bless my putter with good fortune, and I accomplish the unthinkable.
Blessings and happiness follow me, even though awards and trophies
may not always await me.
I shall forever rejoice on the nineteenth green, where my family will
celebrate with me.

# Psalm 37: The Fate of Cheaters and the Reward of the Honest

Do not grow angry with those who are dishonest in their count,
or envy those who knock it stiff.
For as quick as you can spray a shot,
you can also make an eagle.
Put your trust in God and you will improve.
Resting secure on your course, you will fare well.
Take delight in your Guide,
and reserve a place for God in your heart,
for God ultimately grants you your heart's desire.
Commit all your strokes to the divine and be confident.
The gentle Master will be ever present to you.
Stay silent around others and wait patiently your turn.
Do not become riled when a poor player unjustly counts strokes, and
plays unfairly,

for he knows in his heart it is the only way he can win against you.
Be neither angry or upset, as you will lose your concentration.
Instead stay calm and focused and you will ultimately surpass him,
    winning the game.

# Psalm 54: Confident Prayer in the Divine Master

Divine Master, please help me in the skins game,
and with your power and strength direct me.
Hear my plea for confidence as I address the ball with my ginty.
Arrogant golfers may make fun of me; jokesters may try to distract me,
thinking it will throw me off my game.
But you will guide me and keep me focused; you delight when I make it
on the green and reassure me as I try my best.
After each hole I will praise you, for your goodness and love are my
    companions.
You have rescued me from many hazards along the way.
As I trust in you for help, may others look to me for help along the way.

# Psalm 62: Trust in the Divine Master Alone

In my Guide alone does my spirit trust. Each step along the fairway,
my God is there.
God is like the shade against the scorching noonday sun
and like a cool breeze on a sultry day.
God's presence is as sure as a rock on soft ground.

I ask God's pardon for those who never play fair;
I know God watches their every stroke.
How long will my friendly foursome last when rules of courtesy are not observed, or when one drives for show and putts only for dough?
I rest in my Guide, who will see me through.
When the game is over, I will still laugh, for the game was fun even though I may not have won.
God is my shield and safety when I come close to the woods.
God is my strength as my drive went well over two hundred yards down the fairway.
I know God is beside me, always giving me help.

# Psalm 63: Yearning for the Divine Master

Gentle Master, you kindly act as my caddy, though I know that I am your servant.
Like the parched fairway craves water, so I reach out to you for your love and
guidance. Do not disappoint me, for I have nowhere else to turn as I keep moving along the roughs.

As I am about to tee off, I quietly pray for confidence.
As I line up for a shot, I ask for your assistance.

For I trust your guidance; so often you have helped me avoid the trees and
the traps along the way.
I continue to praise you as I walk my path, smiling to find that the ball
has gone
straight down the "right" fairway.

Love and joy radiate within me today as I am playing for fun.
My conversation is light and I banter without any cutting edges.

I know you are with me because my spirit is happy. I am even playing well,
perhaps because I am not taking my game so seriously.

As the day ends and I return home, I replay the game with a happy smile.
I think of the joyful time I have because you are with me.
May I live my life in this same spirit, with thoughts of you always with me
to guide me
and protect me. May I make you proud of the way I live my life as I reflect
to others
the joy you give me.

I realize that you are my leader and guide.
I rejoice with praise at your support and love for golfers.

# Psalm 65: Thanksgiving

Praise belongs to you, Beloved Master,
as we commit our lives to you, for you hear our prayers and respond
    with love.
When we go astray or wander off course,
we know we can turn to you, and
your loving embrace assures us that we are forgiven.
Blessed are those who draw near to you and dwell in your heart.
Like the golfer who is aware of your subtle guidance, we, too,
are often aware of your presence during our walk along life's fairway.
You calm the roaring seas and the pounding of the waves
as our fairway wanders close to stormy waters.
Even those who live near golf's playing fields or dwell at earth's
outer borders notice and respect you.
Rising each morning we bow our heads in reverent gratitude
for your caring love for the hungry and the lonely
as your protective wings watch over them.

# Psalm 85: Prayer for Peace and Justice

Divine Master, you are gracious to your golfers and
all those who walk your fairways.
You bring back our happy spirit when we hit a straight ball,
You forgive us when we wander away from you and
go into the woods; you awaken in us a new spirit,

a spirit of love and compassion.
Restore in us the spirit of peace, where our hearts will turn to you
when tempted to go astray,
May our hearts always listen to that inner voice
as we walk along the course of our life.
May we reach out to all seeking peace and justice.

PART FIVE

# Vision-Inspired Prayers

## Ephesians 3:16–19

I pray that, according to the riches of his glory, the Divine Master will be
more at home in your heart living within you through faith as you continue
    to trust in him.
May your roots go down deep in the soil of God's marvelous love.
I pray that you may have the strength to comprehend, as all God's
    golfers should,
what is the breadth, length, height, and depth of the Divine Master's love.
May you experience this love for yourselves
    though it is so great that you will
never fully comprehend in height and depth, its length and breadth.
May your being at last be filled with the gentle presence
of the Beloved Master himself.

# Beatitudes for the Golfer

Happy the golfer whose drive is firm and aim is straight;
    she will find herself better positioned to reach her goal.
Happy the golfer who repairs his divot; those who follow will bless him.
Happy the golfer who is constantly counseled by the worst player on
      the team,
    for she will make giant drives in patience.
Happy the golfer whose drive strikes the cart path;
    she will find herself far ahead of the others.
Happy the golfer who patiently waits his turn on the green,
    for he shall be blessed by all.
Happy the golfer who is not envious when his partner's tee is halfway up
      the fairway;
    he can rejoice when others do well.
Happy the honest scorekeeper; though he may lose the game, he is still
      a winner.
Happy the woman who in a single shot drives the ball home from the
      lofty men's tee;
    she will be called awesome.
Happy the one whose ball grazes the head of a swimming muskrat and
      lands upon the fairway.
Truly blessed is that person,
    though no one believes the story as it is continually retold.

# The Prayer of St. Francis for Golfers

Lord, make us honest golfers on the course.
Where jealousy appears, help us affirm one another's gifts.
Where unkind words are spoken, teach us to forgive.
Where others doubt their ability, help us praise and support.
Where there is despair, may we give them encouragement.
Where there is darkness, let us be the spark to brighten their day.
And where there is sadness, inspire us to be joyful.

Divine Master, grant that we may not seek so much to be the best player
as to be grateful to you for the gifts and talents we possess;
To be calm when others are upset;
To be respectful to those we walk the course with.
For it is in giving our best that we receive life.
It is in overlooking faults and weaknesses of others
that you will be compassionate toward us.
It is in dying to our ego that we may become the person you intended
    us to be.